1001
DOT-TO-DOT
CLASSIC PINUPS BY
GIL ELVGREN

THUNDER BAY
P · R · E · S · S
San Diego, California

Welcome to *1001 Dot-to-Dot: Classic Pinups by Gil Elvgren*—and an exciting new challenge. To reveal each image, you'll have to join together exactly 1,001 numbered dots. This will take time and you'll need to focus. So turn off the television and laptop—and work carefully as you bring each picture to life.

Make your way through these pages, and you'll learn about Gil Elvgren, who was perhaps the most successful pinup artist of the twentieth century. Certainly, he was one of the most admired. Many tried to emulate him, but as he gained experience, his images became more and more confident and sophisticated. From the 1940s to the 1960s, his images celebrated the beauty of the all-American girl. She advertised Coca-Cola; she appeared on playing cards; she buttoned up her uniform and went to war. An Elvgren girl always has a smile on her face.

Often, it seems like she wants to have fun, too. Fun that may not be innocent, but it's never too forward, either. So when the dots reveal a little more than she intended, don't worry. She's the girl next door and she's got a twinkle in her eye—the same as you. Keep going! In some puzzles, this will be difficult: sometimes the dots are bunched together. To help you, we've used darker colors for the dots and their corresponding numbers. And if you do get stuck, all the solutions are printed at the back of the book.

When you complete a puzzle, there's no need to stop there. These girls cry out for color. Gil Elvgren was a talented artist, and he chose carefully: the color palettes, gestures, and poses were all considered. The result is a painting of a girl who might, at any moment, step out and say "Hi." So join the dots, reveal her smile, and then—who knows?

JILL NEEDS JACK

In the 1940s and 1950s, the all-American girl was probably a Gil Elvgren girl. He created many of this era's most familiar images, quickly becoming so popular that he was known as "the Norman Rockwell of pinups."

LAZY DAYS HERE AGAIN

Gil's talents were obvious even as a young boy. He carved sculptures out of soap, and doodling in his schoolbooks got him sent home more than once, so his parents supported his early intention to be an architect.

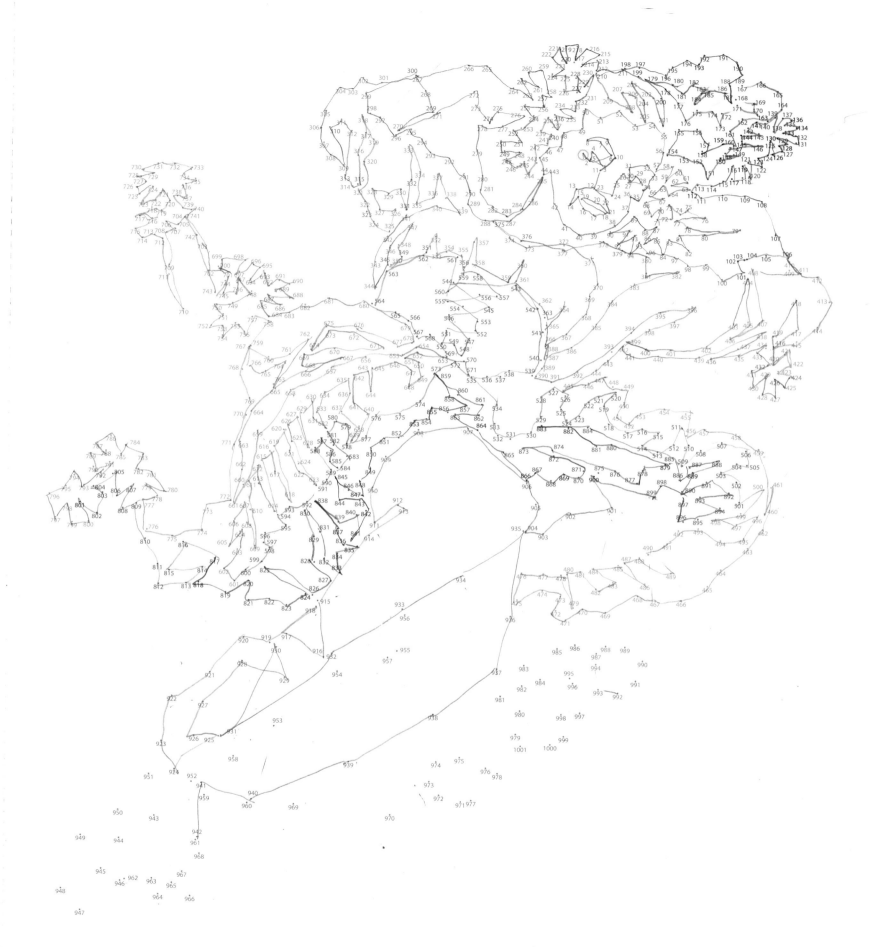

WHAT A VIEW!

Gil enrolled in the University of Minnesota, but he realized quickly that he wanted to make his living from his art. The father of his high school sweetheart, Janet, doubted that was possible, so Gil married her in secret.

MEANT FOR YOU

Upon moving to Chicago in 1934, Gil attended the American Academy of Art. So accomplished was his work as a student that his paintings often featured in the school's catalogs. However, his instructors worried that he might struggle to find work.

BEAUTIFUL LADY

To succeed as a commercial artist, it makes sense to have as many skills as possible. Gil, however, didn't want to learn about advertising layout or lettering. He only wanted to paint, and he took every class he could.

VERDICT WAS "WOW"

Gil packed more than three years of study into just two years, and he graduated early. By then, however, his finances had become strained, and he and his wife returned to Minnesota.

ALL YOURS

In St. Paul, Gil opened a studio and was quick to find work. In 1937 the Louis F. Dow company asked him for a series of pinup girls to reproduce on their calendars. To say his images became popular is an understatement.

ONE FOR THE MONEY

An Elvgren pinup was, and is, immediately recognizable. She always seems like a real person. This is deliberate. Gil preferred working with younger models, who lacked the experience that brings polish but only at the expense of spontaneity.

LET'S EAT OUT

An Elvgren pinup is always a beauty, and she is always approachable: the girl of your dreams and the girl next door. It's a combination that took a lot of planning. First, there was the girl's pose to consider.

A KEY SITUATION

The girl's wardrobe, her props, and the background were all carefully planned.
One further consideration was the hairstyle. The images might be used up to
two years after Gil painted them, so he avoided anything that might date.

CHAP FROM MY LIPS

Elvgren's pinups became best sellers for Louis F. Dow, and when the United States went to war in 1941, the company saw another business opportunity. It quickly produced pinup booklets that could be mailed abroad without an envelope.

KEEPING POSTED

Contemporary photographs indicate just how much of a morale booster an Elvgren girl could be. Images of soldiers in barracks or tents often show a pinup booklet hanging on the wall, or carried in a knapsack.

PERFECT FORM

The war also brought new work to Gil. General Electric commissioned him for their campaign She Knows What Freedom Really Means!, which featured a young woman striding out from home, dressed in the uniform of the Red Cross Motor Corps.

BRONCO BESTED (BRONCO BUSTED)

Gil worked for Coca-Cola throughout the war, and at the war's end, he produced a simple but effective image. A man offers a Coke to a young woman. He may still be wearing his service uniform, but the headline tells us it's "Just like old times."

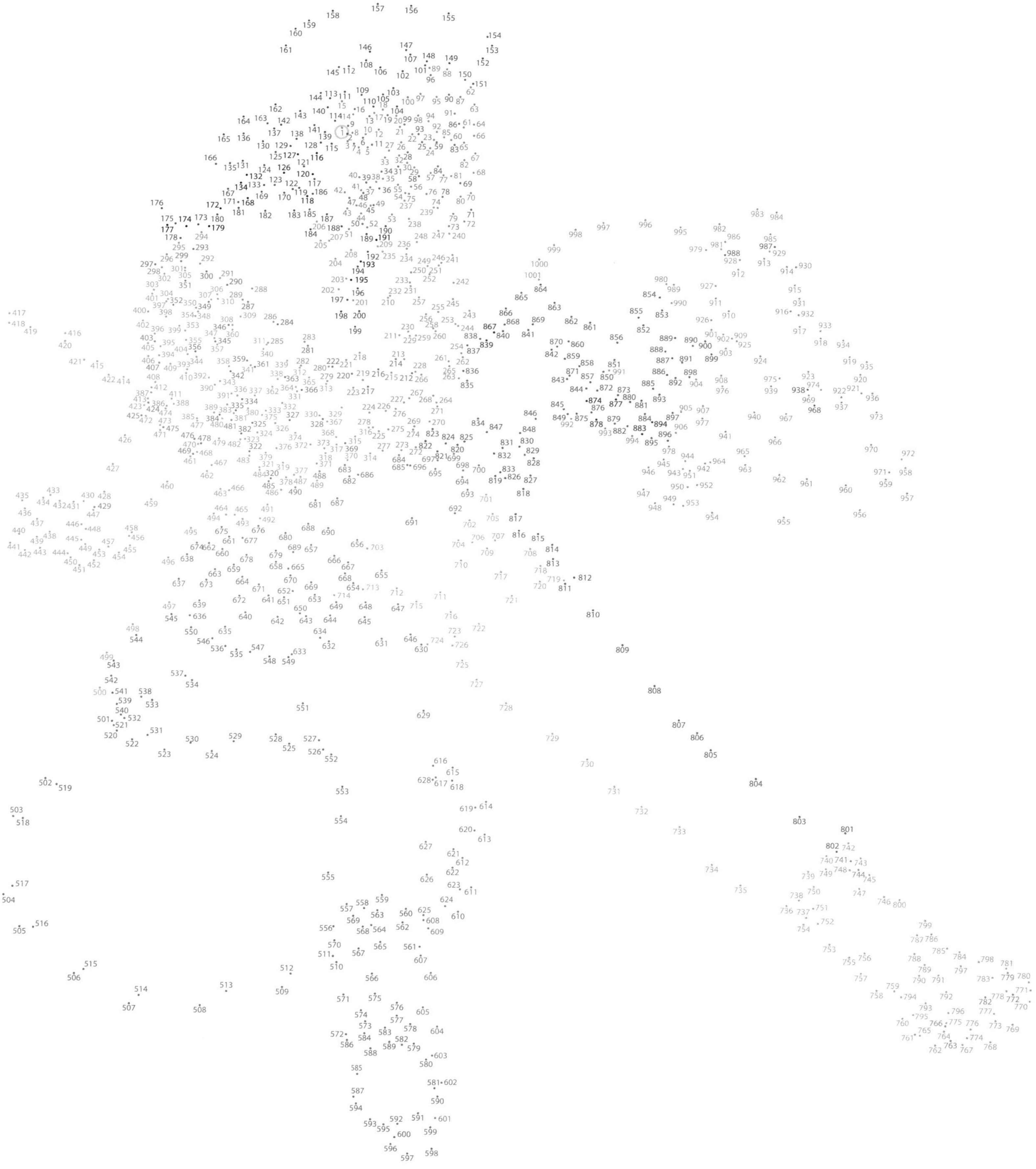

IN THE RED

Gil had been introduced to Coca-Cola by the man he considered his mentor, Haddon Sundblom. The two met in 1940, when Gil moved to Chicago and got a job at the studio that Sundblom had helped establish.

AIMING HIGH

Copying Sundblom, Gil developed a new practice for creating his pinups. Previously, he had worked from a real-life model; now, he carefully posed the model, photographed her, and then painted by referring to the black-and-white image.

POPULAR NUMBER

Today, Elvgren's archives feature many photographs that are *almost* identical to the painted images. So what's the difference? Well, let's just say that Gil used his paintbrush to "touch up." His vibrant golden girls were the perfection of "real" life.

LET'S GO

The pinup girl struck the same pose as the model in the photograph, but her legs were just a little longer, her eyes a little larger, her lips fuller, and her cleavage a little more generous.

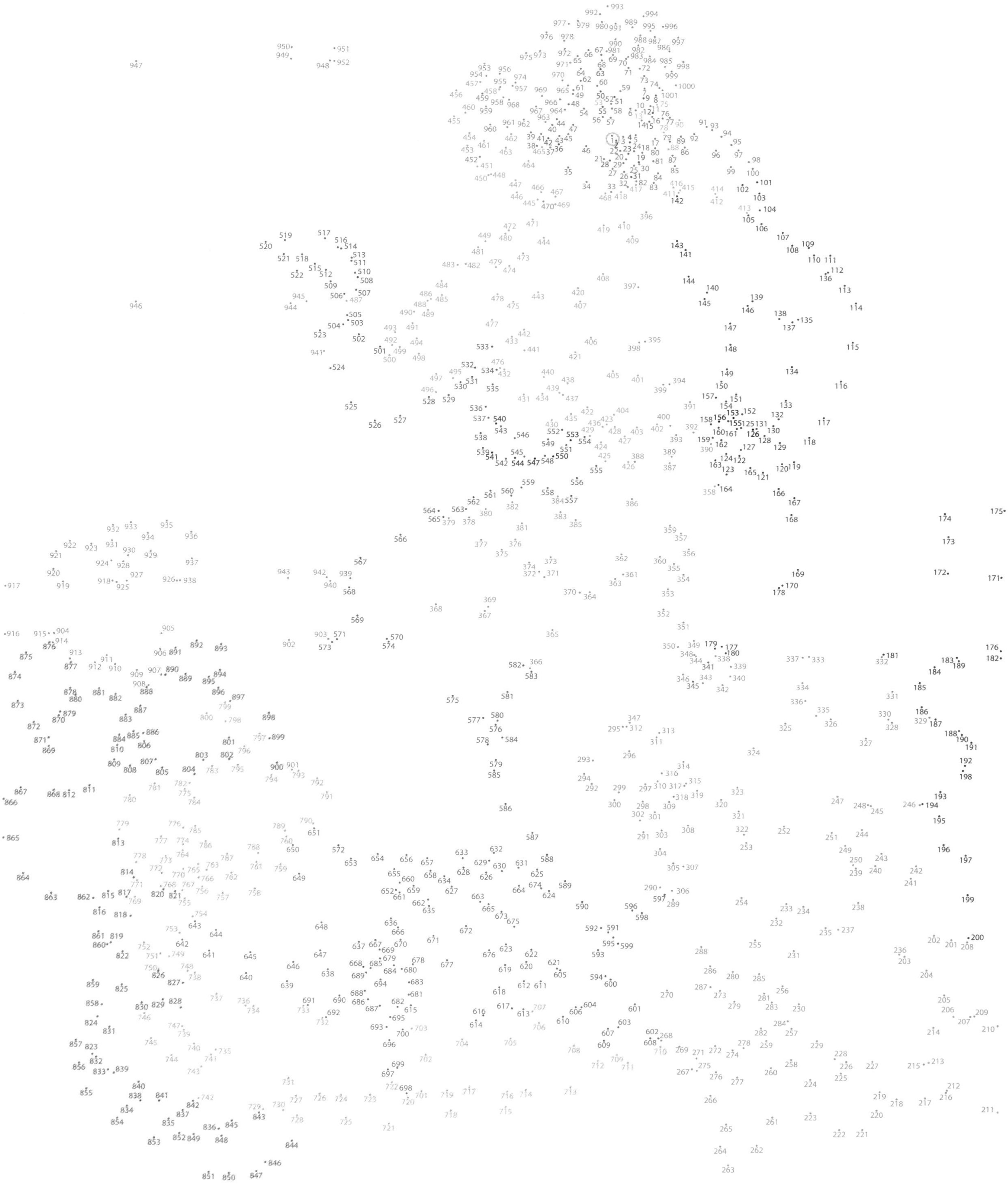

LAST STAND

Gil knew that his pinups were artistic exaggeration, but for him there was always a more important consideration. What he wanted to achieve, over and above enhancing their charms, was a sense of mischief radiating from the girls' eyes.

COMING RIGHT UP

Asked once what he looked for in a model, Gil described someone with a "high forehead, eyes set wide apart, small ears, pert nose, great hair, full but not overblown breasts, nice legs and hands, a pinched-in waist, and natural grace and poise."

DAISIES ARE TELLING

It's easy to assume that Gil's description of the perfect model is impossible for any woman. Look carefully at some of the photographs in his archive, however, and it becomes clear that Gil often asked his own wife to pose.

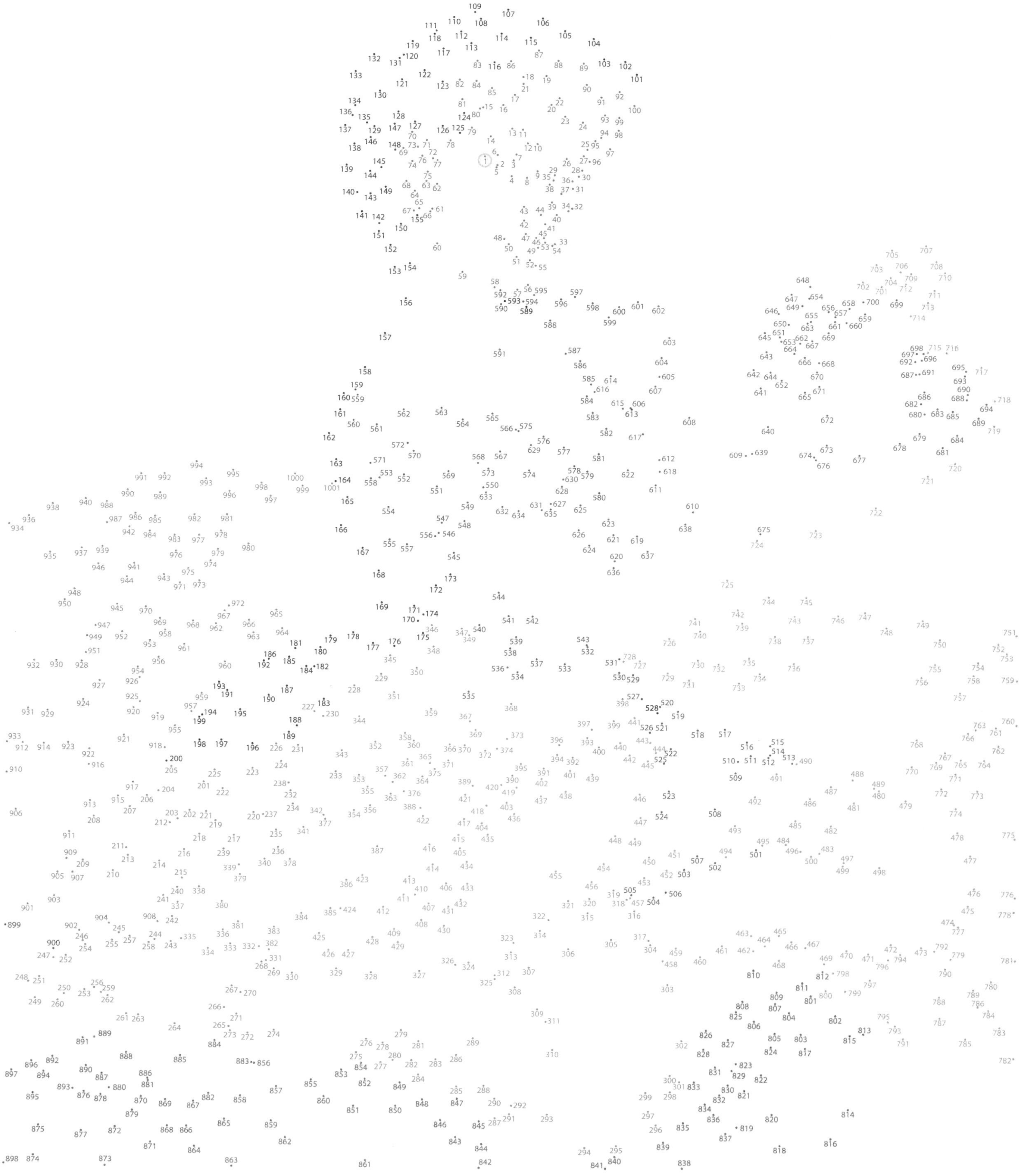

LOOKING UP (QUEEN'S RAIN)

While his wife was pregnant with their third child, Gil received an extraordinary offer. Brown & Bigelow, the most important calendar company in the United States, asked him to work exclusively for them.

FAST LASS (A WINNER)

Brown & Bigelow offered to pay about $1,000 for every painting he created. In his first year, he could expect to earn at least $24,000. Accepting the offer would make him one of the highest-paid illustrators in the country.

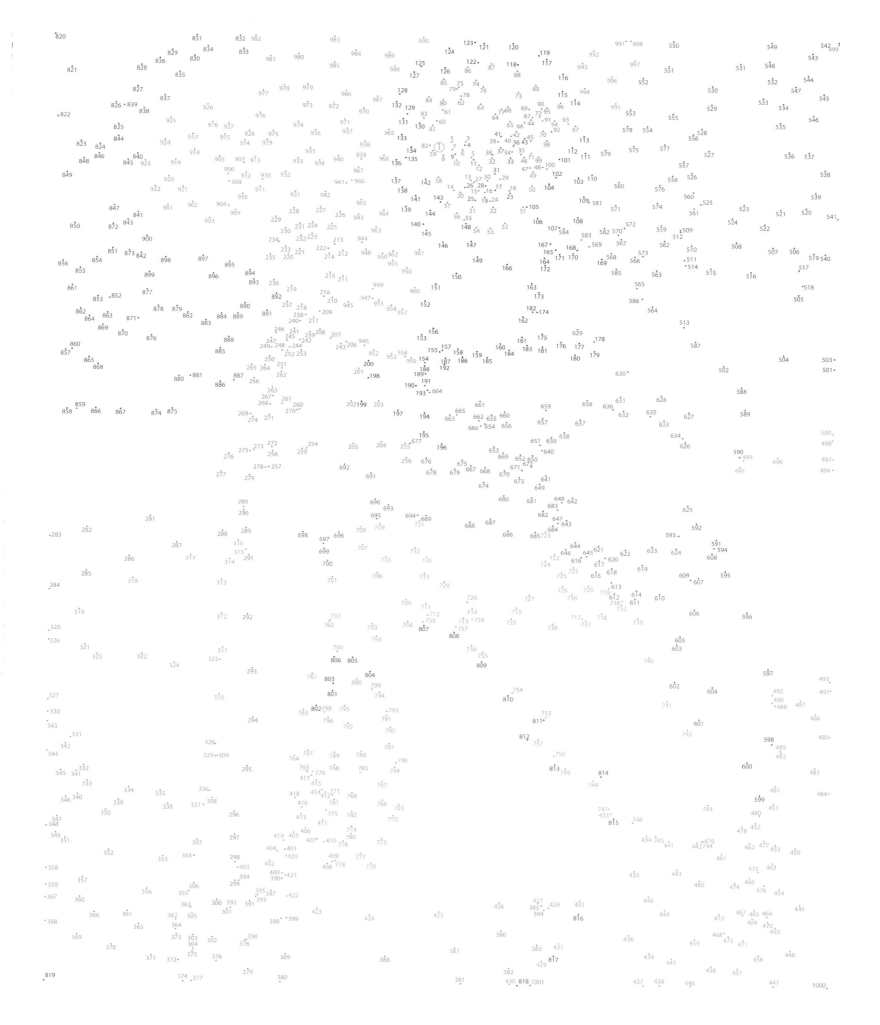

A REAL STOPPER

While Gil considered the offer from Brown & Bigelow, a second commission came his way. Joseph C. Hoover & Sons offered him $2,500 for one painting. *Dream Girl*, the "evening gown" pinup he created, became Hoover's best seller.

I MEET THE MOST INTERESTING PEOPLE

The Brown & Bigelow offer was too good to refuse, and in 1944 he accepted.
Over the next thirty years, he painted at least twenty pinups a year, their sweet
faces and generous curves becoming the epitome of the all-American girl.

SPOTTY PERFORMANCE

An Elvgren girl is never a femme fatale. She is a real girl, often in a real situation, such as turning on the garden hose and picking up her skirts to avoid the water. If she's revealing a little too much thigh, well, that's natural enough.

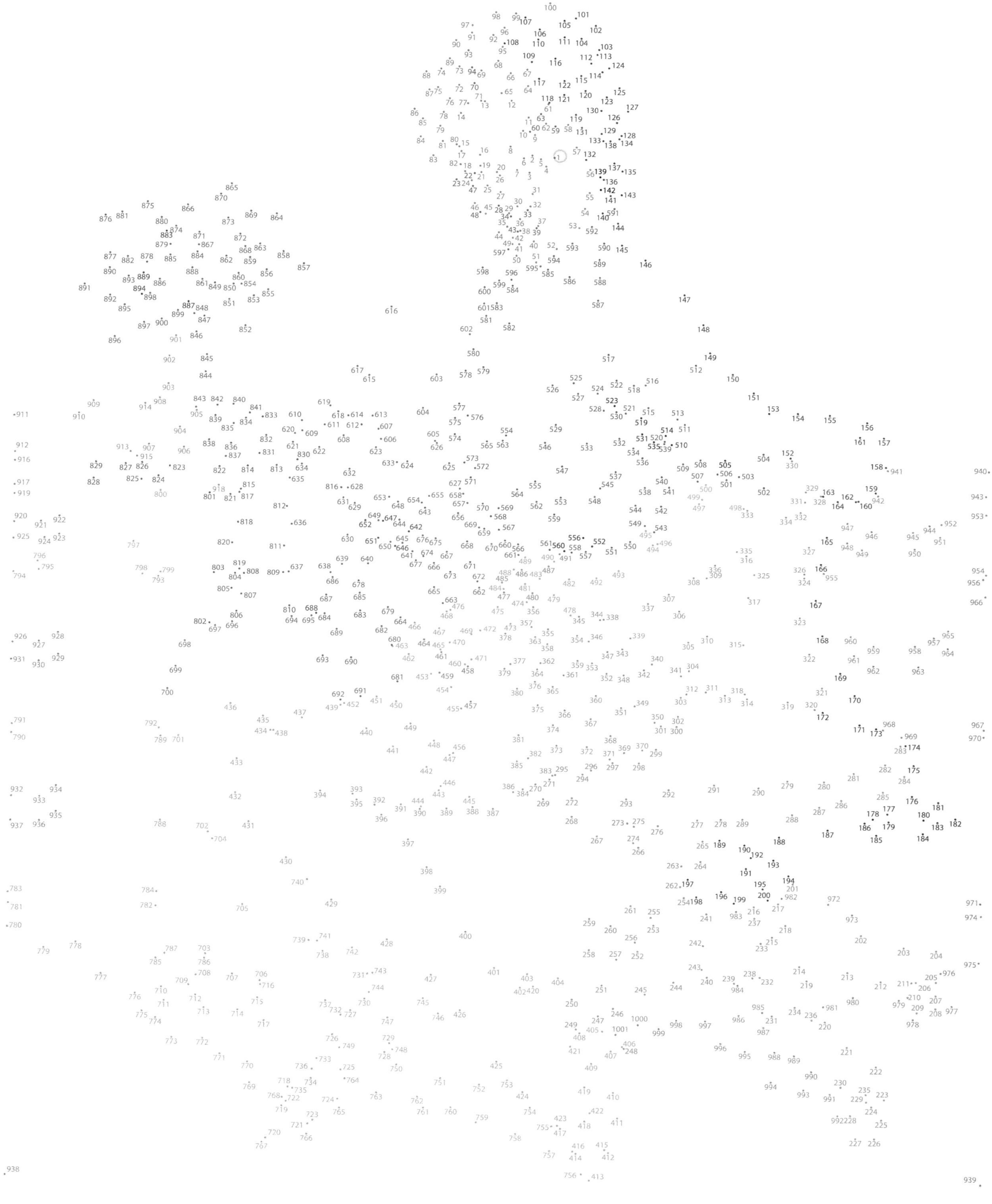

WAITING FOR YOU

When the poses are a little more suggestive, they never suggest sleaze. The dark-haired girl hugging a big red heart in front of her may be naked, but that heart is keeping her modest. Besides, isn't that heart just for you?

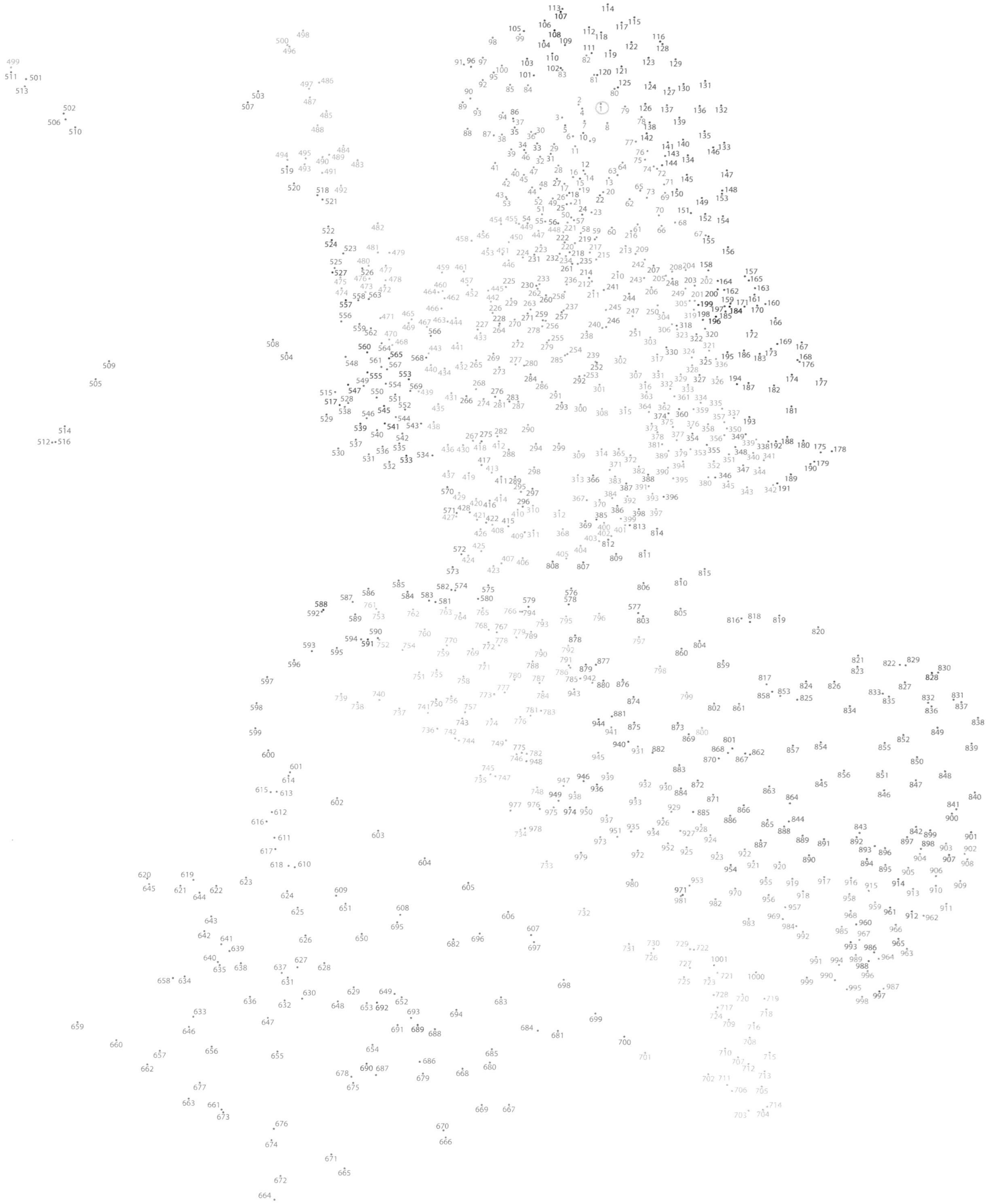

A FAIR SHAKE

The girl in *Sharp Curves* is showing us her suspenders, but those cookies were burning and there were no oven mitts, so what's wrong with using her skirts? As for *A Fair Shake*, she's got work to do. Who cares what you can see?

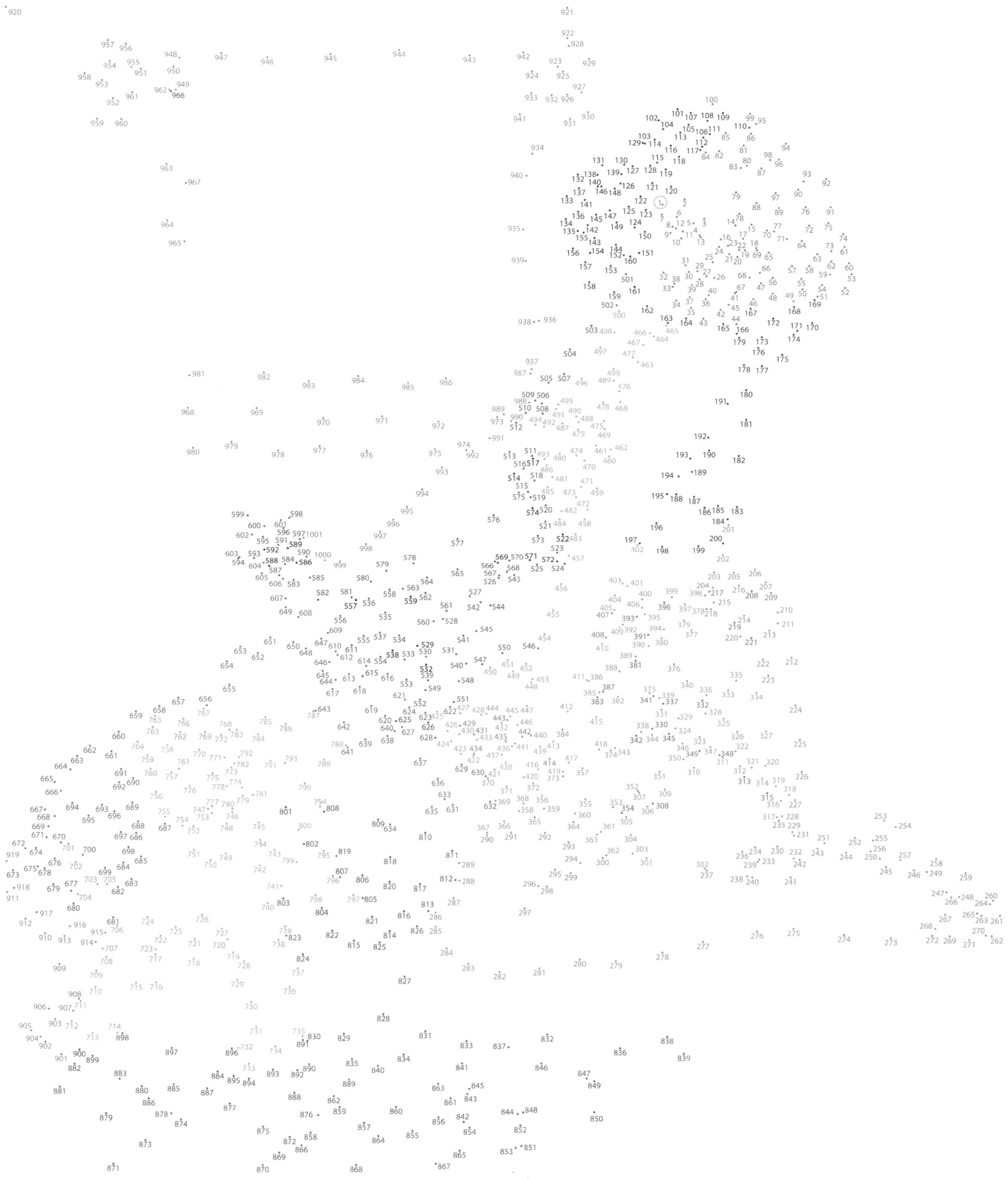

HELP WANTED 1960

It is worth remembering why these girls were initially so popular. Yes, they were sexy, but these were not good-time girls, they were the girls next door. Exactly the type that battle-weary GIs were hoping would be waiting for them back home.

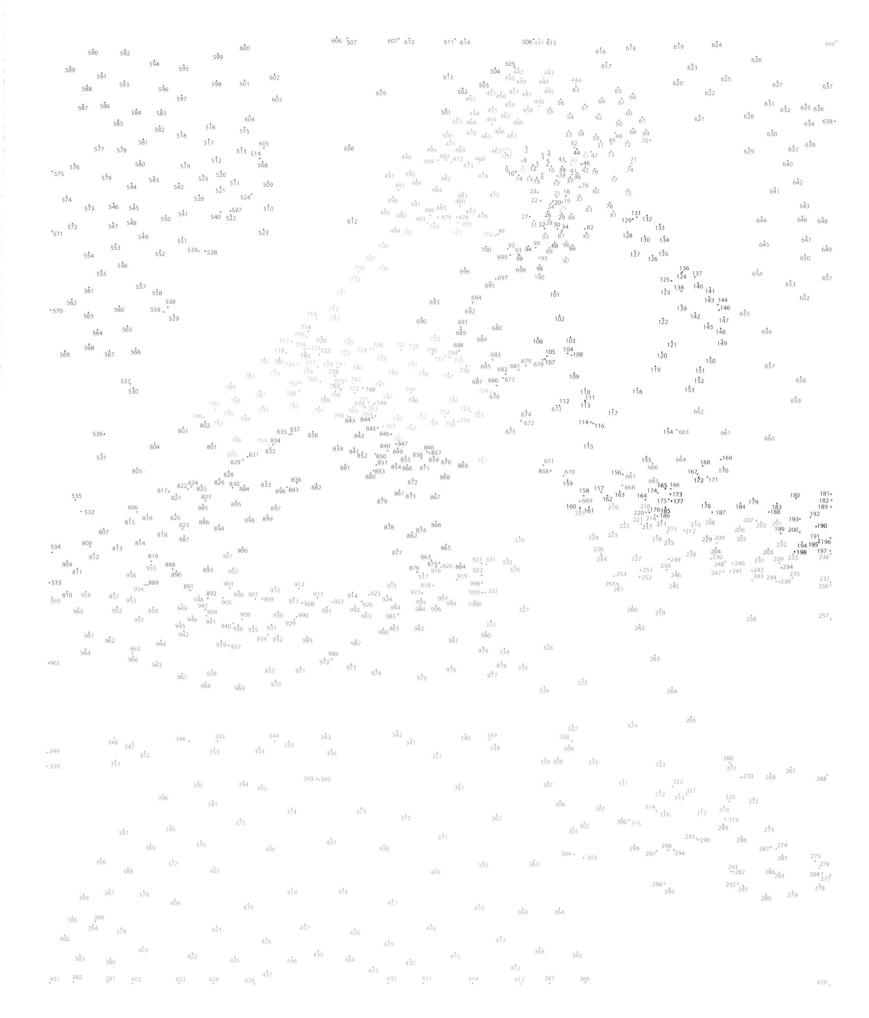

HI HO SILVER

Gil also painted nudes at Brown & Bigelow, although never more than one a year, and sometimes not even that. His first for the company was requested by president Charles Ward, and Gil was eager to please.

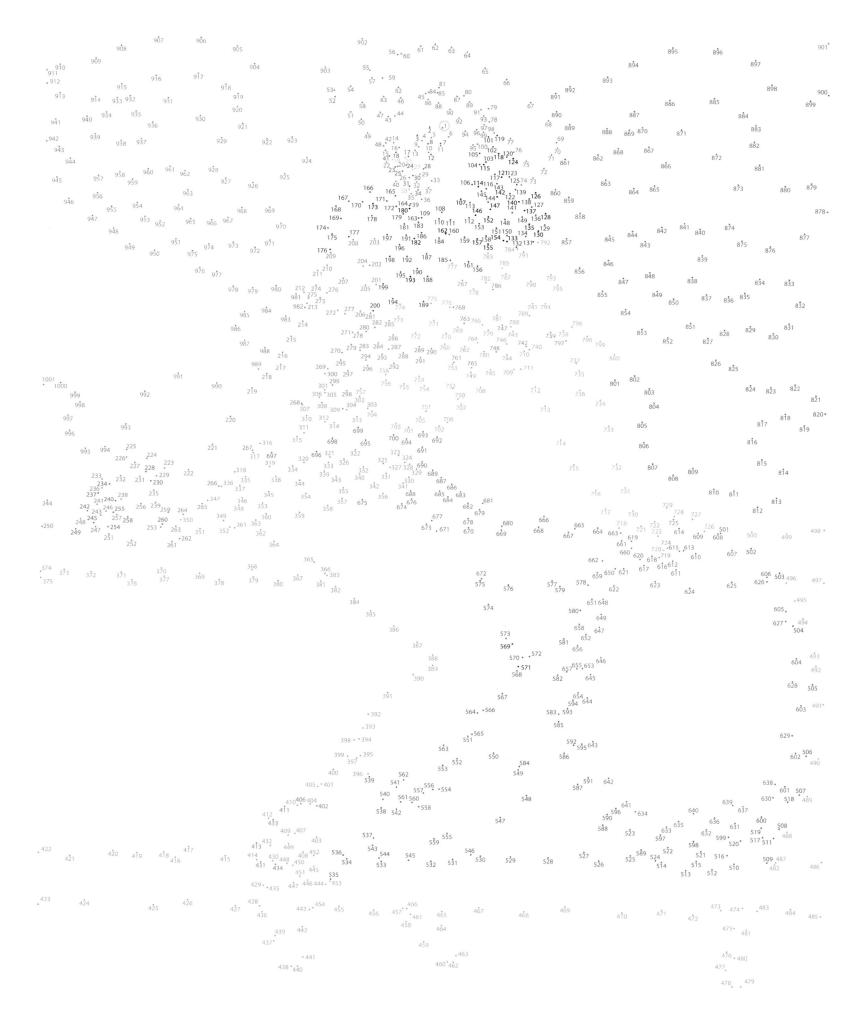

COME AND GET IT

Working on a large canvas, 36 inches by 30 inches, Gil depicted a beautiful blonde on a beach in moonlight. So popular did *Gay Nymph* become, and so quickly, that the company rushed to feature it on a deck of playing cards.

A WARM WELCOME (WAITING FOR SANTA)

Still one of Elvgren's most popular images, *Gay Nymph* sold at auction in 2011 for $286,000. This was more than four times the estimate, and prices for his work continue to go up.

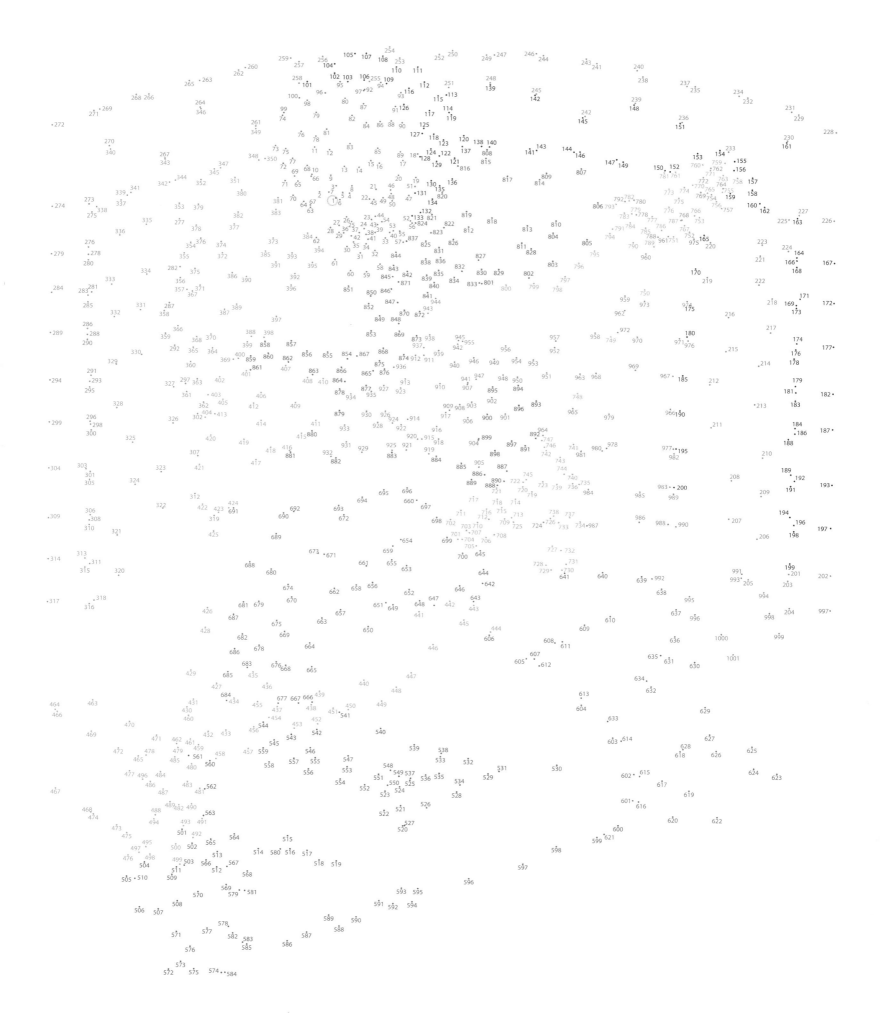

AT YOUR SERVICE

One of the reasons why Elvgren pinups appeal to collectors is that they are complete compositions. Unlike his contemporaries, such as Alberto Vargas, who preferred white backgrounds, Gil always placed his girls in a scene.

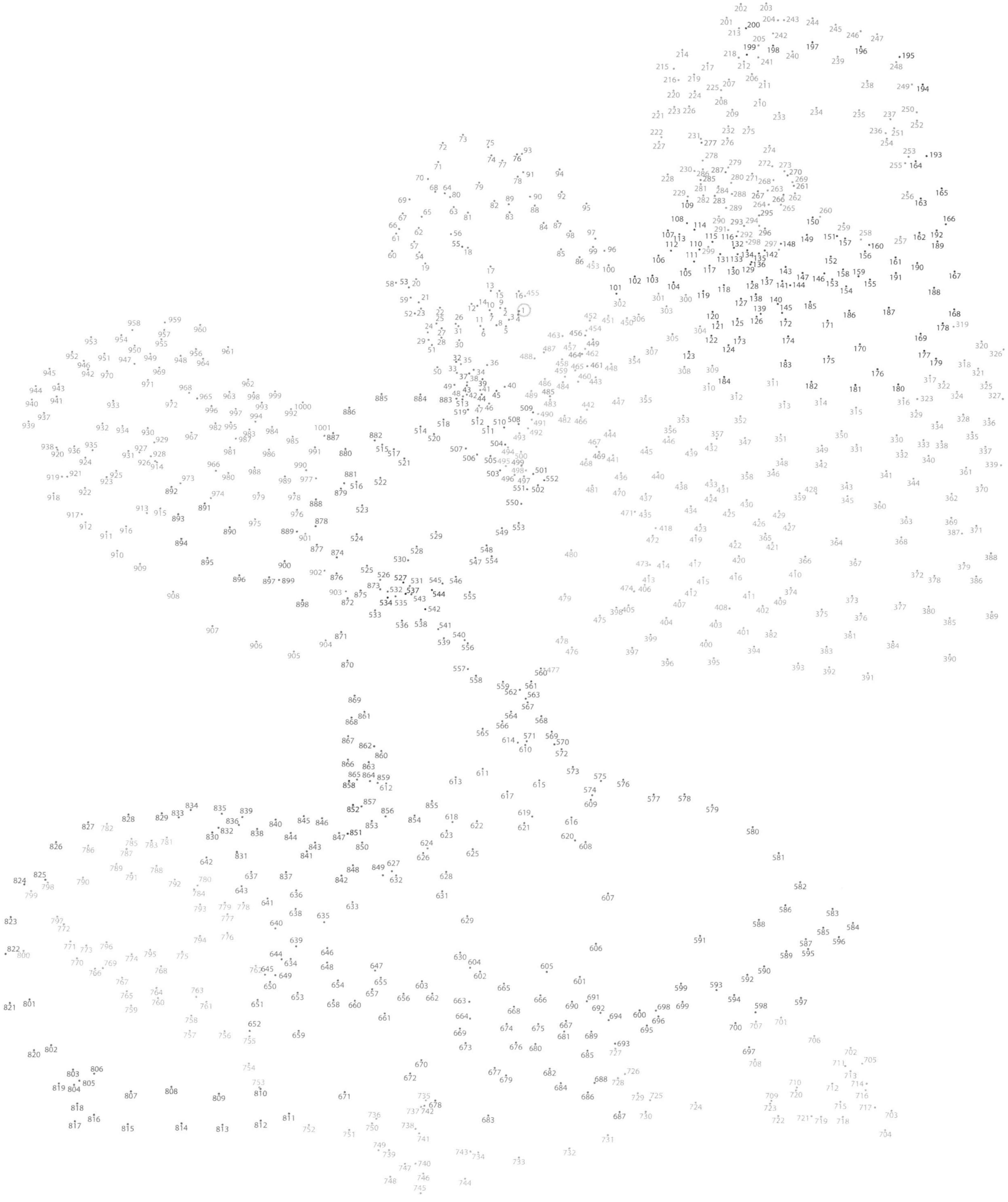

TOO GOOD TO BE TRUE

His paintings often reveal a playful sense of humor, such as capturing the moment when the wind lifts a girl's skirts and the only response is "Oops." Today, these images are popular at auction, as collectors appreciate both the imagination and skill.

ANCHORS A-WOW

Clair Fry, art director at Brown & Bigelow, once explained: "The carefully thought out gestures and expressions are done with such mastery . . . [and] without the phony quality that exists in such a vast percentage of commercial painting."

IT'S A SNAP

Recognizing his skills, Brown & Bigelow was soon promoting not just his work but the artist himself. A letter opener, in the shape of a girl holding a beach ball, was marketed as "Swell gal. Designed by Elvgren."

THE FINISHING TOUCH

Two Elvgren paintings, *To Have* and *To Hold*, were manufactured into a double deck of playing cards. "Whether they be blondes, brunettes, or redheads, gentlemen really prefer GIRLS . . . Especially those charmers painted by Gil Elvgren."

I'VE BEEN SPOTTED

As Gil's fame grew, Brown & Bigelow sent him on promotional tours across the country. Meeting the press and the public must have been hard for a shy man who preferred playing the piano at a party rather than making small talk.

LUCKY DOG

In 1963 Gil received the ultimate accolade: a deck of playing cards called "American Beauties," featuring not one but fifty-two Elvgren girls. No other artist for Brown & Bigelow was ever so honored, and the cards sold well.

AIMING TO PLEASE SHOVING OFF

Throughout his years with Brown & Bigelow, Gil was allowed to take other commissions as long as they did not conflict with his work for them. In truth, his style was so recognizable that the exposure probably benefited everyone.

SHARP LOOKOUT

For Schmidt, he created *Pick of the Picnic*, a smiling beauty holding a tray of bottles. Among the images he created for Coca-Cola were *Delicious and Refreshing*, and *Thirst Asks for Nothing More.* Naturally, the titles refer to the products.

KEEP YOUR EYE ON THE BALL

Gil Elvgren continued working until the day he died. His work always remained up to date. His final commission, for Napa Auto Parts, captures the new fashion of the 1970s: jogging. An Elvgren girl is never out of style.

JILL NEEDS JACK

LAZY DAYS HERE AGAIN

WHAT A VIEW!

MEANT FOR YOU

BEAUTIFUL LADY

VERDICT WAS "WOW"

ALL YOURS

ONE FOR THE MONEY

LET'S EAT OUT

A KEY SITUATION

CHAP FROM MY LIPS

KEEPING POSTED

PERFECT FORM

BRONCO BESTED (BRONCO BUSTED)

IN THE RED

AIMING HIGH

POPULAR NUMBER

LET'S GO

LAST STAND

COMING RIGHT UP

DAISIES ARE TELLING

LOOKING UP (QUEEN'S RAIN)

FAST LASS (A WINNER)

A REAL STOPPER

I MEET THE MOST INTERESTING PEOPLE

SPOTTY PERFORMANCE

WAITING FOR YOU

A FAIR SHAKE

HELP WANTED 1960

HI HO SILVER

COME AND GET IT

A WARM WELCOME (WAITING FOR SANTA)

AT YOUR SERVICE

TOO GOOD TO BE TRUE

ANCHORS A-WOW

IT'S A SNAP

THE FINISHING TOUCH

I'VE BEEN SPOTTED

LUCKY DOG

AIMING TO PLEASE SHOVING OFF

SHARP LOOKOUT

KEEP YOUR EYE ON THE BALL

Thunder Bay Press
An imprint of Printers Row Publishing Group
10350 Barnes Canyon Road, Suite 100, San Diego, CA 92121
www.thunderbaybooks.com

Text © 2017 Carlton Books Limited
Images © Brown & Bigelow, Inc., St. Paul, Minnesota

Printers Row Publishing Group is a division of Readerlink Distribution Services, LLC.
Thunder Bay Press is a registered trademark of Readerlink Distribution Services, LLC.

All notations of errors or omissions should be addressed to Thunder Bay Press, Editorial Department, at the above address. All other correspondence (author inquiries, permissions) concerning the content of this book should be addressed to Carlton Books Ltd, 20 Mortimer Street, London W1T 3JW
www.carltonbooks.co.uk

Thunder Bay Press
Publisher: Peter Norton
Publishing Team: Lori Asbury, Ana Parker, Kathryn Chipinka, Aaron Guzman
Editorial Team: JoAnn Padgett, Melinda Allman, Dan Mansfield

ISBN: 978-1-68412-016-1

Printed in China

21 20 19 18 17   1 2 3 4 5